The Handyman's Guide to End Times

Mary Burritt
Christiansen
Poetry Series

Mary Burritt Christiansen Poetry Series
Hilda Raz, Series Editor

The Mary Burritt Christiansen Poetry Series publishes two to four books a year that engage and give voice to the realities of living, working, and experiencing the West and the Border as places and as metaphors. The purpose of the series is to expand access to, and the audience for, quality poetry, both single volumes and anthologies, that can be used for general reading as well as in classrooms.

Also available in the Mary Burritt Christiansen Poetry Series:

For additional titles in the Mary Burritt Christiansen Poetry Series, please visit unmpress.com.

THE HANDYMAN'S
GUIDE TO END TIMES

poems

Juan J. Morales (signature)

JUAN J. MORALES

University of New Mexico Press ✖ Albuquerque

© 2018 by Juan J. Morales
All rights reserved. Published 2018
Printed in the United States of America

Library of Congress Cataloging-in-Publication Data
Names: Morales, Juan J. author.
Title: The handyman's guide to end times: poems / Juan J. Morales.
Description: Albuquerque: University of New Mexico Press, 2018. |
    Series: Mary Burritt Christiansen poetry series |
Identifiers: LCCN 2018006290 (print) | LCCN 2018009725 (e-book) |
    ISBN 9780826359995 (e-book) | ISBN 9780826359988 (pbk.: alk. paper)
Subjects: LCSH: Zombies—Poetry.
Classification: LCC PS3613.O7155 (e-book) | LCC PS3613.O7155 A6 2018 (print) |
    DDC 811/.6—dc23
LC record available at https://lccn.loc.gov/2018006290

Cover illustrations courtesy of Vecteezy.com
Cover designed by Felicia Cedillos
Composed in Dante MT Std 11/13

For Patti

Contents

III. Inhabitation

I. DEMOLITION

The Long Engagement

Will you shoot bottles with me on weekends shortly after the first reports
of attacks? Will you grimace next to me when the television signals black out
from the dropped warheads glistening on metropolises? Do you promise
to huddle next to the radio with me until we lose all voices to static?

Will you dig the fallout shelter we are not meant to finish, share
wary smiles, and brush ash from my hair too?

I will walk beside you on the rubbled streets and over-stomped fields,
resist picking the only flowers left
for you, kill whatever is edible—in times of rationing and scavenging,
in sleeplessness and dehydration, in fever and epidemic
for as long as we both are human.

Let us be happy adding broken electronics and blunt tools to the Ready Kit.
Promise, even if you don't believe in God anymore,
we will finally have quality time together with our respirators
and we will dance into a life of running
hand in hand through the charred aftermath, counting
our bullets and our blessings, one by one.

A Prayer for Safe Travels

When you leave for good
driving into sunrise, navigating
old highway towns of comfort abandoned,
just know that I'm sorry.
Your courage is packed
to fit in suitcases, boxes, and a truck
that carry the ghosts of our home—
a couch, movies, clothes, the antique desk,
appliances, and half of our books.
I tell you again to be safe,
to breathe in the other side of the country.
Let culture shock transform into your daily lodgings.
Get used to wandering
through a new city full of old churches
that honor little things.
I will conjure your nearness
then release it, and then I will start
putting myself together
with screws and wires and wrenches
somewhere in the time zones
keeping us apart.

Wishes and Dinosaurs

Now I am a dusty professor who neglected
my science and can barely do math,
imagining the part of my childhood I spaced,
the Yucatán's mass extinction crater that left earth
in an asteroid's sable shadow
or the ice age that insinuated the end in one last hit.

I buried toys through the yard and searched
for them days later with sticks that felt
like small picks in my hand, the actual dinosaur toys
always vanishing first.

The trilobite always reminded me of a tank
stuck in the mud. I argued the Allosaurus
could take down the Brontosaurus.
Calling the T. rex my favorite felt too easy.
I was sorry the Stegosaurus wasn't as cool
as the Triceratops, that I didn't know the duck-billed
dinosaur's real name. I wish I were different

and didn't want to step back in time, be a dinosaur
bone guy, rugged explorer holding
the fragments of a former ocean on a Colorado plain,
extracting skeletons from lonely digs
at the end of the world.

The Zombie Sisyphus Dream

Lying at the bottom of
a half-collapsed
room, the floor slanting
on me. I am injured
but I punch and kick
the zombie head.
It tumbles up, pauses,
and then clatters back.
The head wears eyes
that starve, jaw full of
hungry gnashing,
the neck gone except
choice tendons dangling.

There is no boulder to push
upward here. The real hell
is wondering why
I want to stop
and greet my last marvelous error
biting through my clothes,
into my flesh,
and why I never do.

My Eco-Crimes

Forgive me for running the tap too long,
the houseplants murdered, paper towels
and paper plates, brand new light bulbs
dropped, the shabby pens lost,
and house lights left on when no one was home.
Sorry for the now-extinct mice
I killed for living in my air conditioner,
the flowers cut before they went to seed,
fruits and veggies I didn't get around to eating,
the bottles and cans I was too lazy to fish
from the trash. I apologize for leaving
the crust of my bread, for pitching
tinfoil after one use.

But I'm not sorry
for the smokes I smashed out after a few drags
during the countdown toward a polluted future.
I will miss the days of excessive living
with soap or washers and dryers or
radios or wallets or gas stations
from the salad days when I thought
recycling was good enough.

One Last Love Poem

I confess I'm nervous to preserve you
before the little things slip away like lost wishes.
Maybe I'm not ready but it escapes
in a sigh. Before it's too late, before fully waking
from this life, I will write to your body,
to your telling stories. I will drink them into my day
recalling subtle winks
you'd throw across a room. I will always
see the charm of a scar
interrupting your lashes.

If I could, one last time, I would kiss the freckles
and moles you hate, the matching cigarette burns
on your hands, the small knee scar
you never explained. Either way, I can let you
collapse into the calamities
of beauty, when I don't know
what else to say or when I let myself
swirl into other sensations of you
I'm sorry I couldn't hold on to.

I'd like to think I have a photo-sharp memory
but I still hammer down to earth
noticing the strands of your hair
around the house that will vanish in time
and bobby pins I find becoming
mousetraps that snap smaller memoirs,
subtle as your skin beyond perfume.

Ghost Songs

For Mike

He rehearses new melodies
worn on a guitar older than him, but the crowd
always wants old tunes that haunt him
like the debts of heartbreak
that crippled him a lifetime ago.
I'm in the audience, fighting
my own phantom voices, coaxed out
by smiles I can't remember, phone calls I failed
to make, and mistakes in roughed-up notebooks
I can't read anymore.
We share the gut punch
of the saddest notes onstage. We see him glancing
at the spirits of lovers, wearing faces
heavier than any scuffed-up amp.
We hope the ghost songs
finally lose him after the next gig
or across a state line
if he plays through them
to untangle all of our past regrets, knotted up,
one chord at a time.

Secret Maintenance

Home became a tangle of curtains, picture frames, and a flipped-over
   welcome mat.

Home became furniture and linens I didn't use enough,

but still protected with a vacuum, rags, and cleaners.

The house became a monument to screwdrivers, hammers, brushes, and pliers

where I once thought I'd die happy.

Somewhere between the ticks of lonely clocks ceasing, me and my minus one.

I became caretaker for the creaks of the house still settling,

maintenance that secretly devastated me.

Mixtape Ghazal

Back in the day, with a boom box, way back
when tapes and CDs crashed together into every track,

starting with track one, knowing it gotta hook, it gotta rock
and crank into track two, leaving you wanting another track.

I dig out songs you might have lost, out of print,
and hum them so I won't forget to put them as the next track.

The dead air between songs varies, but I want
clean bridges and segues, ready to hit pause for the next track.

I am spinning my history through music, raised
on a punk-ska-rock mosaic. Here's the next track.

Near the end of Side A, I squeeze in songs
until there's no room, afraid of cutting off the last track.

Side B kick-starts patience. Repeat the rewind and retry
past the screwups into another track.

The clicks and hiss come when the music's volume
chops up guitars and bass and drums that riff off the next track.

The bands on my patched-up backpack live on both sides—
always adding bands you must hear. Next track.

It's a little clear rectangle handed off with liner notes,
handwritten to tell you who's next on the track.

Even if a good mix wears out with every play, Juan,
we still share the hunger for the next track.

Turf War

Shooting pool at the Golden Dragon, we'd battle
the Mexican migrants for the jukebox. We were high schoolers,
talking shit about the rancheras they'd played nonstop
and jamming our quarters into the slot for our block
of Top 40 rock, hip-hop, or any tunes we recognized.
They'd glare at us, tired from the construction and landscaping work
we didn't understand yet. We were too scared to talk to them,
but they taught us, from a few tables over,
to play cutthroat without picking the crooked cues and to hum
the entire catalog of Los Tigres del Norte. Close to nine or ten at night,
we accepted our surrender with a humbled nod and promised
to try again next Friday, still pining
for the taste of beer and the last two songs we paid for.

La Ranchera

In the San Luis Valley,
the AM plays a ranchera
where a woman laments losing her lover.
Her ex listens to her pained song
and swallows his jealousy of beer.
My Spanish is not good, but I follow
the strum and horns
that count out her tragedy.

I turn off the radio before it ends
for my hike through the Great Sand Dunes.
When my shoes fill to discomfort,
I empty out the sand. The mountains surround
on all sides of my view. I want to disappear
behind the dunes and peaks,
the desire I had when I was a child
who watched sunsets dragged beyond
Cheyenne Mountain's blinking radio and TV towers.

Back then, I thought faraway places
stayed blocked by a treacherous climb.
I felt the world bigger than where it ended
with nothing on the other side.

I listen to the AM again, driving home
and thinking of la ranchera.
In my head, she's longing for someone
to find her as brilliant as the stars again,
in a future without a broken home.
I am captured in the same melody
with nowhere to direct it.

Across The Overrun States

I'm smart enough to brace for government's collapse,
the great zombie build-up paraded down
the boulevard behind four horsemen in the ozone spewed black
by Yellowstone erupting and the solar storms
shorting out all our circuits, but
there are fears I dodge
in the assumption we'd be together.

There is no plan beyond
the tool bag I should have packed
and a few bottles of water rolling around
in the back of my car
and the lack of courage to ask
if you want me to pursue you at all.

I should check if I have enough lumber to board up
my windows and doors, shaking off
the probability of being an early-on casualty,
but I can't decide if home is where
I take a stand
or if I'm supposed to abandon it.

Poco a Poco

Perhaps I shouldn't hang hopes
on five syllables, three words
caught in my mind, that say "little by little"
on the leaner days,

a song that soothes uproar like

prayers mom and dad speak for me.
Ornate like their St. Christopher medal
carefully pinned in my car, the mantra sails me
on to where I'm from, to where I'm going.

The Cemetery on the Outskirts

The living come with grassy tread
to read the gravestones on the hill;
the graveyard draws the living still,
but never anymore the dead.

—ROBERT FROST, "In a Disused Grave Yard"

A walled-up garden of stones:

markers and crosses felled, slanted

by decades and snow. Somewhere in the rows,

I pass lots too old to be visited, with two names

chiseled in onyx script: *Here Lies Harry Dean Death.*

And also Jane Death. I laugh then stop, startled by

the surrounding graves overgrown

by a ghost-tired hush that seeped sickness

from the Deaths' bones to touch every plot

within reach. I touch their headstone,

peer closer at the dates chipped out.

The stone's chill settles into my hand. I trade

curiosity for a quick exit, away from the dead that usher me

back toward town, alive on the cough of quiet elegies.

Leaving the Carnival

I screamed for the spinning octopus ride
to stop. The smell of cotton candy
was blasphemy all over my clothes.

I didn't stop my mother
when she wiped my mouth
and covered me in a blanket.
She led me through

the flashy night, away from the octopus
with a body
black as the oil pumping gears and sockets.
Its tentacles, with red flesh
and purple suction cups,

craned above. I heard people quiet
when I passed. I prayed
no one recognized me.
Everyone on the roller coaster confirmed
with screams like laughter.

My stomach still teetered.
Children rode the merry-go-round in
woozy circles. Others tossed
rings toward bottles
dreaming of awkward animals fixed on prize walls.

Near the exit, shaped like a craggy volcano,
my mother placed her arm
around me, and we walked in silence,

and the colored lights blinked
like a city on a mountain I could never visit again,

lost in the glare of my watering eyes.

Living the Moth Apocalypse

They bash skulls against
light bulbs and window screens. They help our city's cats
revitalize their predatory instincts with living rooms
transformed into killing floors
cluttered with ripped wings and
the crumbs of a post-apocalyptic diet. But we're afraid this year—

the confusion of moths loving unseasonable heat, intensified
groupings hiding in our clothes, the ambush
of dusted wings with every opened screen door.

We are terrified citizens
filling buckets of water
next to cheap lamps. We break our porch lights
to avoid attracting more and rap
on door frames to scare them into the open. We trap ourselves
at home in the darkness. We end up
like the friend of a friend in the moth-induced

car wreck on our way home,
absurd as our neighboring town
overrun by tumbleweeds last summer.

We kneel before our cats
through the long months of our town's decline,
pleading that they become as swift as
the rainstorms and swallows
cleansing it all away.

Self-Portrait of Handyman Sanding Floors

I disappear under respirator and goggles.
I'm a survivor in a wasteland
separated into dining room, living room,
bedroom one, and bedroom two.
Under my mask, I taste the dust
and blink it out of my eyes.
The sander is a few decades old and weighs
more than I do. It rumbles the floors
then glides, the spinning wheels chewing off the stains,
scratches, and gouges
saved over the last two generations
in the floor that will be swept and wiped
into the soft, honey touch
of an aftermath that lies beneath.

Eating Habits

He wiped it with the cloth and bit into it. Dry and almost tasteless. But an apple.
He ate it entire, seeds and all.

—CORMAC MCCARTHY, *The Road*

I bite into apples
with wrinkling skin, lost crisp,
that brown with every bite.
The apple's wisdom tells me

to stop short
of finishing off
the whole core, so I can always
recall tastes that once
teased my tongue,

the knowledge mislaid
in my gaping stomach.

I practice
for meager times
just in case.

Leaving the First House

I'm not ashamed to admit I've hugged
the walls and even kissed them, in the old '50s rancher,
our first and last house. Its strong bones gave us the want to have

its hints of disrepair and to see its good haunt
in the kitchen doorframe marked with a child's growth
and penciled measurements in nooks and crannies.

We scraped popcorn ceilings, caressed them and the walls
with our own textures, then painted every white room
with warm orange, greens, and bold accent walls.

When we resurrected bathrooms and hardwood floors,
we believed in what our hands could shape, the beauty
of trial and life in the dust of a construction zone

all worth it. Even after five years, I know
I can cry for a place, and even when we go our separate ways,
it doesn't change this home.

How to Dismantle a Mirror

Behind my reflection, I slide
a putty knife to loosen the glass.
I chip through clear epoxy. I pull forward
with caution to extend the rift between
wall and mirror, optimistic
I can salvage it as a single sheet
until the first pop snakes and cracks
up the middle. I fracture it more
as I contort and bend the mirror, still tempted
to explode and smash it all down.

I never looked at myself in the large shards
that could free-fall and make
my vital arteries and limbs
hectic reds as seen in slasher flicks with enough gore
to make me turn away. I've always respected
broken glass and I already have a tab of seven bad years.
I count myself lucky to be sweeping up
dots of mirror off the floor, wrapping then breaking
the bigger flakes into a cardboard box,
and fooling myself into thinking I survived
all the horrors reflected around the house
with only yellow bruises and scrapes
I don't remember placing.

II. REANIMATION

Your New Haunted House

Your buyer's remorse is sanding out
raccoon prints tracked in paint through the kitchen
and out the back door.
You will ask the wallpaper not to pull off
the plaster. You will put hands
in between floors
to replace leaky copper pipes.

You move into your investment,
starting with you
on an air mattress in the living room
until you finish a bedroom.
Then renovate the next room
like young newlyweds who don't believe
in ghosts, oblivious to waking
malevolent phantoms
in the walls and left-behind furniture
stored in the basement.
Except there is no couple.

You're on your own.
Instead of voices piercing the silence
with "Get out,"
they're enticing you
to swallow the bitterness.
You're tempted, but roll up your sleeves
to get your new haunted house cozy enough
to let the ghosts
you brought from the last house
mingle with the ones
already living in the solitude.

My Mother's Daily Phone Calls

after I got divorced were the same.
We summarized our days,
described the sad meal for one
I cooked on my strict depression diet,
my nonexistent plans
for the weekend that culminated
in the long pause before she'd ask—
"Are you lonely?"
My usual reply,
"Not until you asked me."
She followed with stinging worry
for my long nights
in the dark, big house that echoed
of no one else here, and how
I slept in an immensely cold bed,
seemingly larger than nightmares, leaving me
tossed in the sinking feeling inside
that could only be defined
as a heart shattering. I always answered, "I'm fine,"
tone tainted with held-back tears that cataloged
the ways I could off myself that very night
if she kept pushing me.

My mother always called me "Juancito,"
and I'd tell her to ask how I was doing
instead of listing every corner
of isolation. When I could finally say to myself,
"You are ordinary in your failings," I could

honestly tell her I was getting "better."
She worried less and called less,
leading us to future phone calls
where we could speak past lulls on the line
and mock the fear
of dying and living alone.

Driving to Albuquerque

I've made this drive dozens of times,
but it's been years since I last took
the descent
into la frontera
between mountains and desert,
the city where I used to live.

I quiet for Raton Pass
with its charred trees
stripped of leaves and stop
in a Romeroville gas station
with fresh bathroom graffiti.

I sing till it hurts my throat
to new and old tunes cranked
and mess with the visor
where I-25 curves just north of Santa Fe.

I cry for my selfish loss of love
with the Los Conchas Fire growing in the distance,
while a man I will never know
jumps off a bridge outside of Taos.

Approaching Albuquerque, I notice
that the Sandias, mountains I never
gave enough credit, feel more
jagged and lush.
I pull over
to photograph when the sun hits
the range with the right glow
of October blood.

It is a few weeks before my thirty-first birthday
when I return to the Duke City,
another home away from, where everyone
locks dead bolts, no one drinks from the tap,
or leaves their nice shit
in the car, and it's all
an arid version of heaven
I didn't know I missed.

Teaching the Zombie How to Human Again

I wouldn't have trouble stabbing its resurrected brain,
but I'd rather bring it back to who she was.
I restrain her to a dining room chair,
in front of the table with every family photo
I find in the house
to assemble a memory shrine.
Then I lean close enough
for her to zombie me and plead,
"I see humanity in your eyes.
Why don't you remember me?"

Death of an Appliance

When the dishwasher can't clean
through its cycles,
your heart
tightens, afraid to
grieve again so soon after
that meager month you barely survived
the lost washer, dryer,
fridge, and water heater to old age
in your last house.

When the dishwasher's motor skills
sputter and sigh, you resist
punching a wall
and open it up
to diagnose a motor,
to peel past insulation and moldings,
to swap out bolts,
to bond together
parts
with duct tape and superglue.

When you finally fail,
the betrayal of replacing the dishwasher
stings most when it's hauled
to the scrapyard
where misfit
appliances
are sent to pasture, leaving you
shocked to be mourning
a stupid appliance.

Night Watch

The first time I saw a UFO
was after dusk, with my parents
locking the front door before heading to church.
It was a Thursday. I stared past
the yellow hills behind our neighborhood,
above the busy interstate's steady flow
and into the blue evening. The orb,
glowing somewhere between white and yellow,
hovered north to south, paused,
bobbed back, and then zipped into nowhere.

I was eleven or twelve
and couldn't speak up, but I spent
the night marveling what it might be about—
our church in an industrial park, the God
I thought lived in clouds, our planet's
sluggish spin, my own small life divvied
into whatever I could jam into
my pockets, composition books, and play.
I convinced myself the orb knew about me,
so I stuck myself on night watch,
where I have spotted
shooting stars that glowed the sky green
and satellites that blinked along invisible strings,
through more than two decades
of vigil—me in statuary waiting—
for the heavens, angels, alien astronauts, or anyone
to deliver me further instructions.

Scraping the Popcorn Ceiling

Forgive those who sprayed the ceilings,
for they knew not what they did.
Back in the nave of your home, stand
on your ladder, spray then scrape
with the angle that will not stab through drywall.
Mud over it later. Hope it will cover
imperfect trowel strokes,
baptizing it thick with primer paint
and a new color to worship daily.
Fight the dust that sneaks upstairs,
under rugs, and into beds until it cakes to your tired body.
Accept the powder leaking inside
your goggles and mouth as communion
with the ceiling, the burning in your neck and arms
as penance for the sins of the original home owner.
There are no holy relics here.
Be humbled by mud and paint splotches
on your shoes in tribute to the ceiling
you will never admit
reminds you
of a cathedral made with a full week's work.

Children Playing with a Cannonball

We welcomed it
as a gift from the gods and took turns
dropping seven heavy pounds
of smooth cannonball
on our Hot Wheels and Tonka trunks, smashing out
replica windows and popping off
wheels. We converted
our sandbox into a junkyard

with two days of arrogant mayhem
until our parents punished us without a word.
We were left to play with broken toys
and hints of the bigger world out there
that tempted us to destroy
the rest of our childhood
and even more
beyond our cul-de-sac
and the neighborhood water tower.

Breaking the Rules of the Zombie Flick, I

You're in something like a movie
when you turn. You act your part
and groan with the group.
Still wearing death masks,
you all break the rules and hatch
delicious traps for the living.
The whole time, white words overlay
the screen, identifying your former names
and occupations even if clothes give it away.
When you realize you're not undead,
your fellow zombies attack.
They surround you and tell you to give in,
"None of you wasted," they promise
when they dig into where your house of skin
ends and begins. The excess
of blood hurts. They stand over you, satisfied
and ready to corral survivors into food.
The film rolls on without giving you
the chance to wise up
or arm yourself to the teeth.
No rescue, rewind, or alternate takes.

Handyman Checks for Alligators in the Sewer

It was Lennon and McCartney who said all you need is love, and
I would agree with that. As long as you keep the gators fed.
—STEPHEN KING, "Why We Crave Horror Movies"

I descend to where gators must be flushed
after outgrowing novelty houses.
I can smell the bite of violence brewing
in stale water and waste. I am walking
against the rat traffic until tunnels
grow too small, search until the water gets
too dark, the light too weak. I approach
the flickering eyes above water,
jaws flexed. Offering myself to the reptile
that sent me colliding with sweating mains,
I sadly search into the slick grime,
the teeth crushing through the bones change my mind,
tugging me back through the labyrinth of pipes.
I surface and slide the manhole back in place.

You Are Not a Plumber

After seven or more hours of work
to MacGyver a major leak into a minor one,

after water spraying into your face and
two changes of clothes,

after racking knuckles against studs and pipes
and the stress headache's pound,

after three trips to the hardware store
for a washer, hacksaw blade, and Teflon tape,

after cutting the copper pipe
short by one-eighth of a goddamn inch,

after learning sixteen new ways to
thread cuss words together with "fuck,"

after smashing a tape measure
against the floor and gaping a hole in the freshly painted wall,

and after realizing you're out of ideas and willing
to pay a plumber $228 after all,

you feel better knowing that even Bassui
would snap his walking stick in half.

Passive Aggressive

At my angriest, I threaten to leave
dishes in the sink for days, to let the trash stink,
to refuse eye contact,
and to stop saying
"please" or "thank you,"
and then feel guilty enough
to do all my chores in an afternoon.

I'm not afraid to bounce the house awake
in howling tears and
inflict atrocities
on innocent furniture
made of particle board and glue.

If I weren't a nice guy, I would trip
people in line
at the bank, slap a cell phone
out of someone's rude hand, provoke strangers
to pummel me for a few good licks,
refuse a tip for a waiter,
and let my shadow side
parade the streets
in daylight instead and still
end up wishing all of you the best.

Breaking the Rules of the Zombie Flick, II

In this scene, you're stumbling dead toward
two friends and pause
when one looks at you with pity eyes
and guns you down. The hot bullet
drops you harsh as the field
where you lay. Understand it
as a head shot meant to help you out
of this z-world mess. Problem is
you can't speak and you're back on your feet
when the other friend
blasts you through the same head and face
a few more times. You've lost count
and you're annoyed
to be full of failed kill shots, tapped out
of blood, and too stubborn to see yourself
as the nightmare that wanted to,
but wouldn't, die.

The Monster behind the Bushes

The neighbor's dogs are barking
and digging against
the fence. When the animal-control man grabs

the iguana's tail, I expect it
to fall away like arms
tumbling off mannequins.

Lizard whips in defense,
writhes and folds its body, claws into
the arms of animal control.

Patched with discolored skin,
the lizard clutches
pine needles and dead leaves in its mouth.

After the animal-control man
yanks the iguana from behind the evergreen bush
I gasp at the lacerations on his forearm

thick as childhood's red paint
and the stoic calm of the lizard's eyes, staring back
with no remorse.

Alone on the Oregon Trail

I got detention in fourth grade for yelling,
"Screw you!" at
Where in the World is Carmen Sandiego?,
but I don't want to dwell on it.

I want to recall floppy disks, like square plates,
darker than the boxes
packed away in garages. I bank away
fuzzy memories of *Number Munchers*, good for
devouring multiples and prime numbers
with the smiley, green creature
zipping the screen, duping me into learning math.

But I'm still stuck on the *Oregon Trail*, rendered
in pixelated graphics, taking my motley family
from Independence, MO, to the Oregon coast.
I was always the farmer, too young to say,
"I ain't no soft-handed banker," even if I felt it.
I set my meals to meager
and traveled the grueling pace,

never afraid to ford the river
or to sacrifice my oxen, but I felt guilt
killing too much meat to carry
back to my starving family,
with the hunting grounds home to rabbits, squirrels,
and lumbering buffalo keeled over
on the black field with a few sparse bushes.
This was the first time
video games made me laugh at death.

When I died of cholera or if someone else
contracted measles, I always answered,
"Your Mom," or "pepperoni"
when the game asked, "What do you want
on your tombstone?" The real death always came
with a classmate ejecting the disk
before the game ended, more painful
than Manifest Destiny, more fatal
than the broken wagon axle scenario
on the plains of Nebraska.

Inside an Hour

I can figure out which guys on the pitch are assholes on and off the field, like the one vato with the neck tattoos, who drives a different sports car each week, who talks shit to his teammates when they don't pass to him, who can place a precise cross when he shuts his damn mouth, who always mooches water, who gives me a head nod at the Mexican restaurant every time I see him, who pouts and won't chase the ball when his team is down by three or more goals, who searches behind trees on the far side of the field for pelotas he will deflate and stuff into suitcases bound for Chilean orphanages, who once called my team captain a motherfucker after scoring a hat trick and almost sparked a brawl. He's still an asshole, but I learn how he favors his right ankle too, inside an hour, each Sunday, playing pick-up soccer and slowly realizing that maybe I'm an asshole too.

Breaking the Rules of the Zombie Flick, III

You're in an old train station
in the heart of the city
with buttresses, columns,
and wide marble stairways.
It's still early in the game
when you're not supposed to kill the changed ones,
because of a rule you feel inside.
You are facing up to dead ones wearing smiles
sharp with secrets. You're pushing away
grabby ones and smashing down
bitey heads on marble floors.
One bites your Achilles' heel,
and you pull away before teeth break skin.
I can't keep doing this dance,
you think, just as you notice
sunshine through a set of glass doors.
The station is all you have known.
You can't help thinking you'll miss
your special group of undead predators.
You mumble forgiveness to everyone before
walking to the door
and exiting into the rest of the world.

Homecoming

My buddy and I split a joint in the car,
driving around Albuquerque, a trip to memory lane
we think we're ready to take,
past the Middle Eastern grocery store
where we'd get takeout, past the university
where we spent too much time, through the Northeast Heights,
and back along Central. We're two friends commiserating
on how wrecked our lives are back
in our hometowns, unexpectedly crashed out
like shopping carts in a dry arroyo. I make him wander
the antique mall where I bought furniture with my ex,
and he drives past the house he shared with his.

We're sad the city's landscaping hasn't changed in over ten years
and the drivers still don't mind cutting us off.
The high doesn't last long enough to say
something hopeful or even strong enough to fool us
into believing this homecoming can give us
answers to questions we didn't know how to ask.
I char my fingers and snuff out the joint.

Fourth of July

I sealed the
smoke bomb into a bottle
to release a trapped ribbon of blue.
My friends stepped back

to watch smoke expand and swirl.
The bottle bent, swelled
pressured heat that wished to melt
glass back into sand.
The lid trembled until

my eyesight became a large blooming
of a firework show that banged
concussive and threw me
into spiraled sparks,
that fell like a curtain shredded
into night's smoldering black.

I dripped a gleaming blood trail
from the vacant lot,
into the 7–Eleven, up the hill,
and all the way home,
plucking the tinted red shreds

exploded into my face,
learning to cry glass
from the eye that went blind.

Perfume

For Steve Hayward

When the inmate answers with "perfume," I assume
he misses the beauty of a specific woman he lost,
bathed in her subtle scent, a delicate droplet.
I translate it wrong, but he is patient to point out
the correct word in the Spanish-English dictionary.
Not perfume, cologne.

We negotiate the mislaid words between us. We write
in the D Block lounge about how he misses
the bottles of cologne that lined his bathroom window,
how he shaved and then smiled in the struggle
to pick the right essence for the day.

He's soft-spoken but tells me the inside is absent
of smell. He would accept the bad ones over nothing.
When we finish our session, he returns to his cell,
and I am left with a spare poem by an accused killer,
charges that hang over me like a mist.

Handyman Spray-Painting Inside

When I updated my chandelier
with an elegant gloss of black,
I took every precaution
except maybe two or three.

After I spread drop cloths over
the carpet, I would recall later
they should have overlapped the walls.

I shook the can louder than a teenager
pissed off at the world,
worked with even strokes, avoided drips,
and tagged the ceiling only once.

When I picked up the drop cloths to uncover
the uneven shading of beige carpet
now gray, I cursed the diffusion
of spray paint settling the entire room.

After I scrubbed the stained carpet
until my hands numbed, choking on
too much cleaner, I resisted
urges to murder the chandelier and bit

to halt my tongue's wrath. Standing over my graffiti carpet,
before retaliating against myself,
I evoke the handyman's mantra—
sometimes it's just about you
fucking it up.

Nuestra Curandera

For Norma Cantú

In Austin, on crutches with an ankle sprain,
I struggled through city and airport
with a clicking, slow gait.
The poet prayed over me
in a dark lounge with a party murmuring
next door. She placed her hands on
the bruised swell. It hurt
when she told me
this was an old wound
from a past older than me.
I understood how this cost me
a past life and how it balled up
my present pains,
maybe snapped during a murderous chase
or tangled in the chains and ropes of a sinking ship.
I wanted to free my ankle immediately
and take brave steps, but
grating bones and cartilage told me
to walk through the lingering limp
and let it heal.

Standing against the Trees

Because the elm must be lonely
in a field's wintered landscape,
featured in the tree poems I routinely see
in a journal that's rejected me five times.

Because the tree stands for decline
and the nobility of aloneness, I resent it.

I've talked my share of students out of tree poems,
especially the ones featuring a tree house they feel
guilty outgrowing. These are my selfish aversions.

I've cut down the evergreens, dying in the middle,
but I never thought to eulogize them.
I'm not the hippie
who offered to do odd jobs but refused
to cut them because they were still alive, man.

Maybe I'm wrong and the poems and the trees
are one. Maybe that's why I'm afraid of them burning down
and taking me out in the process.

III. INHABITATION

My First Zombie

Every night, it wanders up the dirt road
winding above my old hometown. My family is inside
with my sick mother, who rests in a bed
in a strange new house. I wait in the garage
with a machete—like the one my father
gave me when I turned eighteen.
In the driveway, the skeletal corpse claws forward,
singing out its appetite; I meet it with the simple rule
of lose the head and it's dead
with one surprising swing.
Ligaments severed, no blood, and
body separates. I relax until head reattaches
and the zombie rises to attack again.
I repeat the ritual of decapitation
too many times, and the head always
reattaches. The last time, trembling,
I pick up the head that's staring, breathing,
biting air. I feel its absent soul. I cradle the heavy head,
bringing it away from my family
into the eternal woods, and lose myself in the pounding heart
that throttles dream. I'm always waking up a grown man,
turning on every house light, opening every door,
and startling my mother with phone calls
about wicked weather and lurking questions
about remission, examinations, and her old lamp
with an orange shade
that she does not remember as well as I do.

I Could Be So Lucky

I could be so lucky to have the chance to learn
your many smiles through different seasons,

to memorize your silhouette at the campfire
telling stories you lived before I was around,

to call the end times a choose-your-own-adventure,
to reach for your chilled hand for warmth,

to trust enough on a journey toward an El Dorado
where we could sleep more than two hours,

to sweep already looted convenient stores, joking about
how aspirin and Band-Aids can fix a bite wound,

to stay in earshot but still catch you glancing back after we separate
in search of firewood and water,

to find a lot of abandoned cars hauntingly beautiful,
to greet your lips with mine the first and many times after,

to play a game of "Count the Helicopters and Airplanes"
with neither of us scoring a point,

to have you ask me about what makes me feel safe,
and to hear you hum a few bars of an REM song

we would adopt as our very own anthem,
but I haven't found you yet.

With No End In Sight

You wake from dreams of the evangelist
who bought billboard ads across the country
and picked today ripe
for the reckoning,
so you greet the day walking barefoot,
to your mailbox in your intact neighborhood—
no burned-out cottonwoods,
no doomed message looping on the radio,
no streets congested by resurrected dead,
no spires of smoke climbing over
the city's collision sites.

Cloudless skies document
nothing happening. You're embarrassed
you believed the end was here.
You're uneasy, overcooking breakfast,
brushing teeth two minutes,
slipping on slacks, ironed shirt, and tie
when you ask the world to sigh
with you just this once.

Later, you drive past the evangelist's billboard
with a newly predicted end date.
Like a paring knife that nicks your fingertip,
you concede to hurt that thins
a little more every morning.

Standing on Top of the Interchange

I'm hating the moaning dead nonstop.

I'm tired of the chase I give them. I understand

bridges will outlive us as

cement monoliths

sinking under

the desert where it's best to walk at night.

Growing up, we called these types of roads

spaghetti bridges, but we never felt

their height inside the car.

Back on the edge, with a wincing smile, I bite down

on memory

of what I've done to survive and

back away from the ledge.

Thinking about Duchamp's Urinal

When I install the toilet, I flirt with painting
"R. Mutt, 1917" on the side.
I'm tempted to make statements
about conceptual challenges against normative art,
but this project doesn't advance
my artistic ambitions. It doesn't invite guests
to discover a new interpretation.
I'm more concerned about fitting the porcelain god
in place without cracking it
and keeping the pipes and fittings
free of leaks. Everything else
I flush away.

Our Hieroglyphics

After "Placa/Roll Call" by Chaz Bojórquez

The canvas holds the alphabet
of people tagging where the city hurts
in cholo calligraphy.

The faded black
from an extinct spray can makes
blunt *A*'s, the *O*'s, and *D*'s

that could be triangles,

the smeared curves
in the *E*'s and *Z*'s and *N*'s.

We can see future aliens unlocking
the letters, but will they know
the embedded names

of the aliens today
that hide in the open

and in the slow invasion of two

languages locked in
the crash of ferocious gridlock?
We must now speak

with the hiss of paint,
disrespecting walls with hieroglyphics
that remake our home turf.

Handyman Imagines the Battle of Pueblo

When everyone has turned to biting
each other, to emptying
every grocery store in town,
and to sieging out the end times,
we don't know why we didn't leave
for the mountains in our eyeshot.

Our feet got dirty enough in vacant lots
and beat-up streets
with road cones coaxing us
to leave this rest-stop town.
The heat challenged our souls to keep it together,

hopeful for afternoon rains to nourish
gardens hidden in
Bessemer backyards. We used to feast
at east-side taquerias on one-way streets.
We used to bike through the avenues to slip

downtown, through alleys
graffiti fresh, finding our way
to where the river paralleled limestone barrens,
and levee murals
for local gods that once stretched into sunset.

We want the mill to spew yawns all night,
coal trains to whistle, crashes of train cars
loading again,
so we fortify and clear out
the dead,
to make this town home again.

Like Teens

Excited and anxious, we try
not to glance at the door
every two minutes
before the second one of us arrives.

We share drinks at the bar
with the jump of anticipation leaning us in,
our hands locking.

We discover each other on dates,
making out in the car
an hour after we said we would
go home.

It feels rebellious, newly born
to the world
after losing the giddiness before
to mortgages, work hours, and
nonsense we don't recall.

We text with emoticons to make up
for days or hours
we wait between
the good-byes and everyone asking,
"Why are you smiling?"

You and Me in the Zombie Flick

You tell me that you'd be a survivor,
smart enough to stay out of the way.

I peg myself the second guy
to figure it all out,
who picks up

the key and opens the heavy door
before being swallowed up

in the undead-stuffed corridor.

We omit the promise of wasting

each other
and kiss good luck
before our fight against
a horde of ex-people

devouring toward us.
I think a thought as secret as the tiny

bite wound I hide:
I would end you
if the village depended on it.

You'd do the same
for me.

Watching the Paint Dry

You gifted wall gashes with spackle,
hoarded your best mistakes in this room.
You edged the borders. Went to town
on corners. Muscled roller strokes
in belief you didn't need painter's tape.
Smudged a wet rag to delete
evidence of your wandering mind,
or where cats rubbed against the fresh wall.
You washed everything off your hands.
Maybe it's the epoxy latex smell
that says, "Swim in this color."

The Great Flood

It sounded like someone taking a shower
when the water heater's seam popped
to unleash enough water
to snap a prideful town's houses and bridges
into shambles
of muddy brown.

We thought about vengeful deities sending
awesome waves.
We drowned mops. We littered the floor
with dirty towels.

We smacked wrenches against
the empty tank in vain.
We stood in
wet clothes, guiding the Shop-vac
on the soaked rug,
trembling mad when touching soggy drywall
with defeated hands.

We cleaned
every angry inch of the basement
on achy knees and wished
for time to stockpile
soggy books and blankets
like animals
huddled in an ark,
adrift at sea.

Jellyfish

They pull through currents in large blooms.

A minefield of tendrils armed with marine stingers.

Crowds of them parade past beaches, below boardwalks.

They swarm herring and salmon schools to bits.

Like the surprise of starfish in North Atlantic seas or

glaciers' hairline cracks spilling into slush,

they float amid the most remote sparks in our minds.

Washed ashore, fed by the ocean's dead zones,

they nourish the absence of bones, eyes, and heart.

We aren't afraid enough to notice.

Boy Scouts vs. Zombies

In my elementary school gymnasium,
Scout Master tells us
to do our civic duty
with sharpened sticks
and pocketknives we aren't supposed
to know how to use.

There are no merit badges
for this.
We are never prepared
for teachers and adults possessed
with the undead gait
that rips through a school
full of children.

If I survive, I will join
the future of a living hell,
rebuilt by orphans
who sob for forgiveness to
hungry-for-flesh
mothers and fathers.

I don't want to wear
this uniform anymore. I don't want to be
loyal to my den
or a good citizen
by putting down
our bitten-up Scout Master,

my absent mother,
or reanimated father.
I will pretend
I get a pin for this.

Explaining Seafood to My Future Grandkids after the Extinction

I will describe, like a murder,
how we used to rip open
juicy bodies and clacking claws

of lobsters and crabs
to feast on warm meat inside.
I will smack my lips, describing

how we seared tiny ones with red tails,
called shrimp, in butter, garlic, and batter.
I will contaminate the moment by

describing cocktail and tartar sauce as red or white.
I will explain how the ocean's snakelike wonders
called eels were bendable monsters

made only of arms and fish
who swam in nimble clouds
up and then down to the depths

where deep-sea creatures created their own light
in a time when the sea
was not stung full of jellyfish and

swirling garbage,
and we swam with the taste
of salt pressed to our lips.

Rips

I think in cuss words when I am enlisted
in the war against wallpaper, a losing battle
to the past-era vinyl.
There are no hearts and minds to win—
only hideousness affixed to drywall.

All faiths teach forgiveness,
but I cannot absolve the bedrooms' chrysanthemums,
kitchen's herb and veggies, and
the mother-flecking seashells
and birds flying the garish silver and gold
of my nightmares.

I may forever smell
like wallpaper remover,
but I refuse to establish a new legacy of glue and paper
even if my children look on
my styled age with
shame and embarrassment.
I will fight on with scraper, trowel, and brushes
heavy with primer and paint.

To the Kissing Lovers in the Vancouver Riots, 2011

I wasn't invested when the Bruins shut out the Canucks 4–0
in Game 7 of the Stanley Cup, but gas-can anarchists and fans
rioted for the home team choking in the clutch, or just for the sake
of breaking shit. One lingering image, the viral one, with riot police
sweeping the smoky orange street
and the out-of-focus cop behind a riot shield,
accents the twenty-something couple
lip-locked, him lying on top of her in the middle of the street,
oblivious to the scene. I read the harrowing story
of the two prodded and pushed to the ground
among the arrested looters and licks of fire.
The boyfriend, still wearing a backpack, kissed her into comfort
against pavement.

Even if I declare it bullshit and stagecraft, I still admit
maybe a long, improvised kiss could inspire any of us to lay ourselves
in front of a police line that rolls right over,
to bash away the outraged hockey fans and bored kids,
who do not smash the cameras. Maybe it preserves us
as lovers, you and me in a moment of stillness,
all of us wanting to be saved
from somewhere inside the city's padding heart.

The Stars Are Always Pretty on this Drive

You say this on New Year's Eve
on the way home after we danced ourselves
into nonstop kisses.
That night into morning
we witnessed a falling star
so big it fooled us into thinking it
fireworks popping the sky awake with green.
Every year blinks faster and faster
like the desert labored
into a metropolis in two decades.
How we ended our first one—
stopped on the roadside, intent
on the extra stars jarred awake,
refusing to yield to the cold.

Praise for a Finished Job

Harbor away *HGTV* resentment
for using tools you will never afford
and for stockpiling workers.
Your pipe no longer leaks,
and you can't find where you burst
then repaired the wall.
Because you've hidden it like a pro,
you can stop singing out f-bombs.
Your hands clicked your home apart
and rebuilt it like Atlantis resurrected.
Admire the glow of a small victory.

Ecuadorian Couplets

In times of crisis on the road with a busted car,
in the terminal with eight-hour layovers, and in

a place we couldn't translate, we kept our spirits
up with our smiled mantra: aventuras.

When the tide recedes at dusk, we walk past children
playing tag, all the way to the sunset and back past our

footprints and thousands of sand dollars burying
themselves, pausing to kiss and admire hungry waves.

Driving on Dramamine and coping with the zigzag
mountain roads, we sleep to accelerate arrival. We survive

the town full of three-wheeled taxis with the main street
closed for a soccer tourney, the village where we bought

pan de yuca, the procession carrying their saint along the
road's shoulder, and the stabbing Andes all around us.

On the road outside Baños after hiking the maze of bridges
and waterfalls, we stop on the shoulder to watch Tungurahua

erupt. Billows of smoke darker than the sky. We let it steal our
breath when fire and lava awakens what we will never see again.

✖

We drank agua loca on our last night, my cousins mixed jugo
de mora straight into the bottle. We passed it in a circle, taking

big swigs—the fire down the throat until the bottle
was drained. They told you, "You are one of us now."

To Dream in Spanish

Practice as an adult with phone calls
to mamá y papá. Volunteer to teach
ICE detainees in the jail every Tuesday.
You finally take trips
to the motherland and the fatherland
as a tourist ironically surrounded
by family. Describe your life
back in America with sentences
as simple as charades laced
with off target syntax and cognates.

Give yourself credit when people ask
if you speak it. Don't worry about
your white boy accent. Say yes
instead of the long answer
about not being raised on Spanish
and how you heard
your parents talking it like secrets.

It's okay to fry your brain
code-switching each day in a country
that is not yours.
You won't catch every phrase. Let go.
Fall into the dreams, en sueños,
heavy as rivers overflowing
with accents and tildes,
when you forget you don't speak Spanish
only for the night.

My Love for You

My love for you is a zombie's arm,
smashing through the splintered door,
flailing and grabbing to find you.
It is tired from slamming against walls
but it will never give up
until nothing stands between us.
If you lop it off, be gentle enough
to take out the rest of me.

For the Tiled Floor

We hacked out a straight line
in the hardwood floor.
You cut and patterned tiles
so they tessellated
like the birth of a galaxy
in the palm of your hands.
We leveled the flooring,
mixed mud, and grouted tiles
with precise gaps between
this two-month challenge. We agreed
that we can build a home in a land
where everything malfunctions.

We Kept Meeting

I scour the background
of photographs and memories for you—
maybe a bookstore, a friend
of a guy I knew's band,
a rowdy party along the river,
or in the same line at the coffee shop.
I was the guy in the green jacket you noticed
the night I heard you sing
"Crimson and Clover" at karaoke
when I wasn't drunk enough to
sing "Say It Ain't So."

I'm waiting to uncover more
stories of our crossed paths,
shocking like the summer
I painted the house next door
to where you used to live.
I'll still sneak glances for you
in photographs, but I want to keep
staring forward into you.

Z Harmony

When you're undead, the compatibility parameters expand.
You're caught in the rot of your own bag of skin
with one ravenous mouth and two hands
to claw down a kill.
You now mass with others like you
and no longer worry about
first-date jitters, ordering a dish with garlic,
how long to wait before you text or call, or narrowing
the field one nervous coffee at a time.

If only old instincts could fire up brain cells again
to yearn for the one who could fall
for your unique bite wounds and scratches or look past
the dab of victim on your face
that defines the new you,
the one in a staggered gait missing a shoe.

You were once the guy she could teach
to use chopsticks, who always opened the door
or offered the crook of your arm during a walk,
who could follow her to a favorite clearing
with a blanket to watch for falling stars, but now
love starts by sharing screaming flesh
captured in chase,
playing it hungry, almost confident.

You don't have to worry anymore about her getting tired of your jokes
when you moan out to your undead match,
the one to share harmonious wanderings
toward brain binges, the one you wouldn't have found
in the herd unless you died first. You've adapted together
even if you cannot tell her how divine she looks tonight,
or how somehow, in her tattered, reanimated body, she glides.

Acknowledgments

Many thanks to the editors of the following publications, where some of these poems appeared, sometimes in slightly revised forms:

Acentos Review: "Mix Tape Ghazal"

Catch-Up: "Fourth of July"

Eleven Eleven: "The Cemetery on the Outskirts"

Hayden's Ferry Review: "With No End in Sight"

Imaniman: Poets Writing in the Anzalduan Borderlands: "Our Hieroglyphics"

Ink and Letters: "For the Tiled Floor"

Kweli Journal: "One Last Love Poem"

Luna Luna: "Wishes and Dinosaurs"

Malpais Review: "Leaving the First House" and "Handyman Checks for Alligators in the Sewer"

Manifest West: "Driving to Albuquerque"

Mas Tequila Review: "The Stars Are Always Pretty on This Drive" and "Nuestra Curandera"

Nature and Environmental Writing: A Guide and Anthology: "Explaining Seafood to My Future Grandkids, After the Extinction"

Origins: "To the Kissing Lovers in the Vancouver Riots, 2011"

Ostrich Review: "Inside an Hour"

The Otter: "I Could Be so Lucky" and "Ecuadorian Couplets"

PANK: "Passive Aggressive" and "My First Zombie"

Pariahs Anthology: "Turf Wars"

Pleiades: "Night Watch"

Post Road: "Self Portrait of Handyman Sanding Floors" and "Handyman Imagines the Battle of Pueblo"

Snakeskin UK: "My Love for You"

Sugar House Review: "Boy Scouts vs. Zombies"

Terrain.org: "Alone on the Oregon Trail" and "Jellyfish"

Taos Journal of International Poetry & Art: "La Ranchera" and "To Dream in Spanish"

Zingara Poet: "My Eco-Crimes"

Much appreciation to Daphyne Jillson, Jonathan Bohr Heinen, Gary Jackson, Lisa Hase Jackson, Kirsten Allard, Tom Wiederrecht, Casey Bozell, Scott Gage, Andy Jones, Alysse Kathleen McCanna, Izzy Wasserstein, Liz Derrington, Idris Goodwin, Felicia Rose Chavez, Steve Hayward, Mike Clark, Danny Rosen, Kyle Harvey, Sherwin Bitsui, Rigoberto González, Rich Yañez, Francisco Aragón, Ben Sáenz, my teachers, my *Pilgrimage* familia, and all my friends that surround me with community.

Abrazos fuerte to my CantoMundo familia, "Pintura / Palabra," Con Tinta, Mary Szybist and my workshop mates at the Palm Beach Poetry Festival, and Tupelo Press's 30/30 Project for giving me the community and space to discover and draft many of these poems. Thank you to my talented students, friends, and colleagues at Colorado State University–Pueblo. Thank you to everyone who helped me revise and edit this book: Maria Kelson, Melody Gee, David Keplinger, Iver Arnegard, Juliana Aragón Fatula, Kevin Prufer, Hilda Raz, Elise McHugh, and everyone at UNM Press.

Finally, love to my family: Mom, Dad, Esther, Eric, Sydney, Regan, Morgan, Glenn, Rosita, Rafael, Gwyneth, Thais, Carmen, Alex, Leonard, Karen, Carrie, the Freemans, the Garners, todos en Ecuador y Puerto Rico, Alyssa, Carrie, and Patti, who inspires me beyond words.